SPORTS SUPERSTARS

AARON JUDGE

By Anthony K. Hewson

WORLD BOOK

Your Front Row Seat to the Games

*This edition is co-published by agreement between
Kaleidoscope and World Book, Inc.*

Kaleidoscope Publishing, Inc.
6012 Blue Circle Drive
Minnetonka, MN 55343 U.S.A.

World Book, Inc.
180 North LaSalle St., Suite 900
Chicago IL 60601 U.S.A.

Kaleidoscope ISBNs
978-1-64519-034-9 (library bound)
978-1-64494-190-4 (paperback)
978-1-64519-134-6 (ebook)

World Book ISBN
978-0-7166-4336-4 (library bound)

Library of Congress Control Number
2019940053

Printed in the United States of America.

TABLE OF
CONTENTS

CHAPTER 1

All Rise

Aaron Judge takes his place in right field. The sun shines down on the green grass. Fans in the stadium look on to see the next play.

Suddenly, the ball is coming his way. Judge springs into action. He races back toward the wall. His eyes never lose sight of the ball. Then, using his whole 6-foot-7 (2.0 m) frame, Judge stretches out and grabs it. His 282 pounds (128 kg) go crashing into the wall. But Judge holds on.

Judge is big. He looks more like a football player. But he is an outfielder for the New York Yankees. And this August 2016 game is his Major League Baseball (MLB) **debut**.

Yankees fans had high hopes for Aaron Judge when he arrived in the majors.

FUN FACT

Only two players in baseball history were taller and heavier than Judge. Both were pitchers.

Judge blasts a home run in his first MLB game.

Judge steps to the plate in the second inning. He towers over the catcher. Few MLB players have ever been so tall. Judge had played football in high school. His future in that sport appeared bright. But he stuck with baseball instead. He is about to show why.

Judge watches the first pitch go by. Strike. He fouls off the next pitch. Then he takes a ball. Finally, Judge gets a fastball. He twists his giant body. The bat hits the ball squarely. There is no doubt about it. The ball lands 446 feet (136 m) from home plate. Home run!

NICE STARTS

Teammate Tyler Austin also made his major league debut on August 13, 2016. He hit right before Judge in the lineup. And he also hit a home run in his first at-bat. Two players making their debut had never done that before.

Judge celebrates with his teammates in the **dugout**. But he is not done for the day. Judge singles to left in the fifth inning. Then he comes around to score. Judge is a quiet guy. He doesn't say much. He sums up his big day very simply.

"What a day," he said. "That's all I can really say."

And Judge's career is just beginning.

Yankees teammates congratulate Judge on his first home run.

CHAPTER 2

A Miracle

Aaron Judge crouches down. He raises the bat behind his head. The sound of cheering fans echoes in his head. He's not a major leaguer yet. He's just a kid. Aaron likes to pretend he is on the San Francisco Giants.

The Giants are his favorite team. They play 100 miles (161 km) from his home in Linden, California. Aaron is playing Little League. He swings the bat. It's a home run! But he still has a long way to go.

Aaron dreamed of playing for the San Francisco Giants.

FUN FACT

Giants shortstop Rich Aurilia was Aaron's favorite player as a kid. Aaron even copied Aurilia's batting stance.

Aaron was born April 26, 1992. He had a pretty normal childhood. One day when Aaron was around ten years old he noticed something. Aaron glanced at his parents. They looked different than him. He asked them why. They told him he was **adopted**. Aaron's brother was adopted, too.

Aaron was adopted when he was just one day old. "A miracle," his father Wayne called it. Aaron was not upset when he found out. He just wanted to know.

Aaron excelled at sports. His parents supported him. As teachers, they also made sure he did well in school. Whatever it was, they wanted him to work hard at it.

FUN FACT
Aaron's parents were teachers. His older brother became one, too.

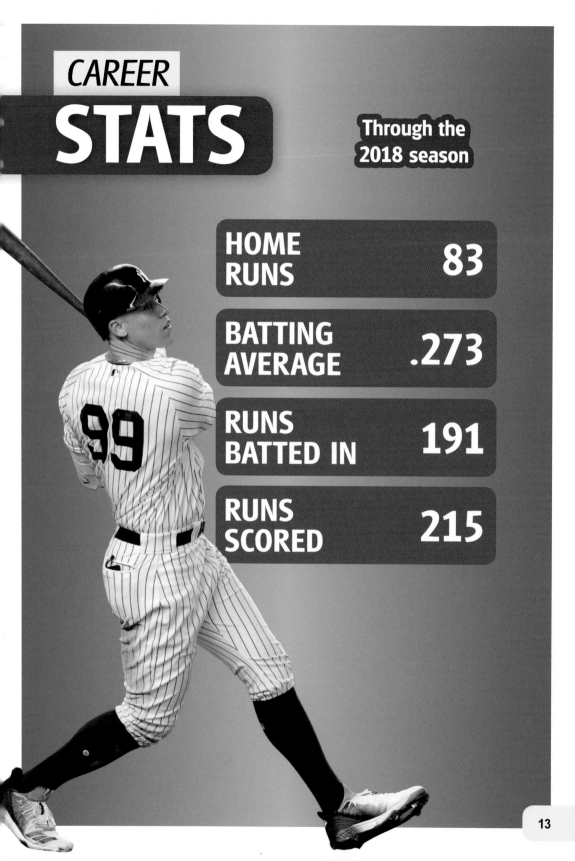

CAREER
STATS

Through the
2018 season

HOME RUNS	83
BATTING AVERAGE	.273
RUNS BATTED IN	191
RUNS SCORED	215

Where Judge Has Been

- **1** **Linden, California:** Judge was born here.

- **2** **Fresno, California:** The home of Fresno State, where Judge played college baseball.

- **3** **Charleston, South Carolina:** Judge made his pro baseball debut with the Class-A Charleston RiverDogs here.

- **4** **Tampa, Florida:** Home of the Tampa Yankees, where Judge played Class-A ball.

- **5** **Trenton, New Jersey:** Judge played Double-A ball with the Trenton Thunder here.

- **6** **Moosic, Pennsylvania:** Judge played Triple-A ball for the Scranton/Wilkes-Barre RailRiders here.

- **7** **Bronx, New York:** The Yankees play in this borough of New York City.

Aaron played baseball, football, and basketball in high school. His dad stood 6-foot-3 (1.9 m). Basketball was Wayne's favorite sport. He was one of few people who could match up with Aaron on the court.

Aaron was a star in all three sports. He could have chosen any one. Colleges were **recruiting** him to play football. But he liked baseball the best. He played at Fresno State.

Wayne came to watch Aaron's college baseball games. He was hard on his son. In one game Aaron got hits in four of five at-bats. Wayne wanted to know what went wrong in the other at-bat. Aaron did not always like this approach. But it pushed him to be a better player.

The New York Yankees agreed. They selected Aaron in the first round of the 2013 **draft**. Wayne was with him for that, too.

Aaron began his pro baseball career with the Charleston RiverDogs in 2014.

CHAPTER 3

Gentle Giant

The Yankees record the third out. The inning is over. Judge trots in from right field. He waits for the other eight Yankees. It doesn't matter what the score is. It doesn't matter how many runs the Yankees allowed. Judge will be waiting. He'll offer a friendly word. He'll encourage his teammates. Once they're all off the field, he joins them in the dugout.

Judge is known as a great teammate. He is there for the other Yankees when they are struggling. His positive attitude helps everyone relax.

Yankees teammates know they can count on Judge for encouragement.

FUN FACT
Judge had baseball's best-selling jersey in 2017. Then he did it again in 2018.

Judge signs autographs for fans before a 2017 game.

FUN FACT

In 2017, a special cheering section opened in Yankee Stadium called "The Judge's Chambers."

Judge has a caring attitude toward others, too. He learned from his parents how to treat people. Judge saw how they helped kids as teachers. Judge works to stop bullying in schools. In 2018, he joined the #ICANHELP campaign. It aims to stamp out online bullying.

Judge also spends a lot of time practicing. He takes lots of swings and hits lots of balls. **Repetition** is huge for big-league hitters. The MLB season is long. Players must keep doing the right thing day in and day out. Judge takes that to extremes. He has a few things he does every single game.

NO. 99

No. 99 is an uncommon number for a baseball player. Only 15 MLB players wore it before Judge. Judge did not choose the number. It was assigned to him in spring training. He decided to stick with it.

It's gameday. Judge pops in two sticks of bubble gum. If he gets out, he throws the gum away. But as long as he gets hits, he keeps chewing. The gum will eventually lose its flavor. But that means Judge had a great game.

Before each game, Judge walks to home plate. Sunflower seeds click together in his hand. He tosses forty of them in the grass behind home plate. Each one represents a Yankees player. He says a prayer and wishes them all good luck.

Routines, such as chewing bubble gum, help Judge stay at the top of his game.

CHAPTER 4

All-Star

Aaron Judge hasn't forgotten. Every day, he looks at a note on his phone. It reads ".179." That was his batting average in 2016. That was very low. No other Yankees starter hit under .200. Judge never forgot that number.

"It's motivation to tell you don't take anything for granted," he said.

Judge points to the sky after hitting a home run in the 2018 playoffs.

Judge stood off to the side of the field. Justin Bour was at the plate. Bour hit one home run. Then another. Before long he had hit 22. Now it was Judge's turn to top him. This was the 2017 Home Run Derby. Judge wasn't nervous. He was there to have fun.

The crowd booed him. That's because the Marlins hosted the event. Bour played for Miami. But Judge silenced the fans with a 427-foot (130-m) blast to center. Judge went on to hit 23 homers. That was enough to win. He went on to win the entire derby. The homers came all season. Judge hit 52. He was named American League (AL) **Rookie** of the Year after his first full season. Only one player had more votes for MVP.

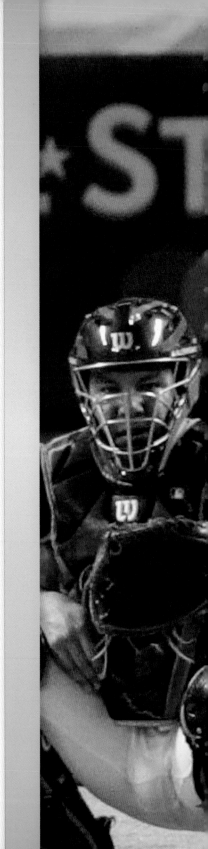

FUN FACT

If strung together, Judge's 47 homers at the 2017 Derby would have traveled 3.9 miles (6.3 km).

Judge goes for another home run at the 2017 Home Run Derby.

On July 26, 2018, the Yankees faced the Kansas City Royals. Judge was on track for another great year. He stepped to the plate. The pitch was up and in. It was 93 miles per hour (150 km/h). And it hit Judge on the right wrist. He shook his hand and cringed in pain. He had to leave the game. He found out later the wrist was broken. Judge did not return until September.

Now it was playoff time. Judge came to bat in the first inning. He launched a two-run homer to left. That was all the runs the Yankees needed. They beat the Oakland Athletics. Judge hit two more home runs in the next round. The Yankees lost. Still, Judge's future was as bright as ever.

Judge, right, and Giancarlo Stanton celebrate Judge's home run in the 2018 playoffs.

CAREER TIMELINE

1992

April 26, 1992
Aaron James Judge is born in Linden, California.

2010
Judge is drafted in the 31st round by the Oakland Athletics. He chooses to play college baseball at Fresno State instead.

2010

2013

2013
The New York Yankees select Judge 32nd overall in the MLB Draft, and this time he signs.

April 3, 2014
Judge makes his pro baseball debut with the Charleston RiverDogs in the minor leagues.

2014

2016

August 13, 2016
Judge homers in the first at-bat of his MLB debut against the Tampa Bay Rays.

July 10, 2017
Judge wins the Home Run Derby, becoming the first rookie to do so.

2017

2017

2017
Judge leads the league with 52 home runs and wins the AL Rookie of the Year award.

2018
Fans vote Judge to start in the All-Star Game. He hits a home run in the game.

2018

2018

2018
After missing parts of the season to injury, Judge hits three home runs in five playoff games.

BEYOND
THE BOOK

After reading the book, it's time to think about what you learned.
Try the following exercises to jumpstart your ideas.

THINK

THAT'S NEWS TO ME. Chapter One describes Judge's first career
MLB home run. What news sources would have covered this event?
What new information might those sources have? Where would you find
sources like that?

CREATE

SHARPEN YOUR RESEARCH SKILLS. Where would you go in
the library to learn more about Judge? Who could you talk to? Make a
research plan to find out. Write a paragraph that details how you might
go about learning more.

SHARE

WHAT'S YOUR OPINION? Chapter Three states that Judge is
considered a great teammate. What evidence is given to support that
opinion? Share this opinion and evidence with a friend. Did he or she find
your argument convincing?

GROW

REAL-LIFE RESEARCH. This book contains a lot of facts about
Judge's career. But there are other ways to learn about someone. What
real places could you go that would tell you more about who he is and
what he does? What else could you learn at these places?

RESEARCH NINJA

Visit *www.ninjaresearcher.com/0349* to learn how to take your research skills and book report writing to the next level!

RESEARCH

DIGITAL LITERACY TOOLS

SEARCH LIKE A PRO
Learn about how to use search engines to find useful websites.

FACT OR FAKE?
Discover how you can tell a trusted website from an untrustworthy resource.

TEXT DETECTIVE
Explore how to zero in on the information you need most.

SHOW YOUR WORK
Research responsibly— learn how to cite sources.

WRITE

GET TO THE POINT
Learn how to express your main ideas.

PLAN OF ATTACK
Learn prewriting exercises and create an outline.

DOWNLOADABLE REPORT FORMS

Further Resources

BOOKS

Bankston, John. *Aaron Judge*. Mitchell Lane Publishers, 2018.

Bates, Greg. *Aaron Judge: Baseball Star.* Focus Readers, 2019.

Lajiness, Katie. *New York Yankees.* Abdo Publishing, 2019.

WEBSITES

Factsurfer.com gives you a safe, fun way to find more information.

1. Go to www.factsurfer.com.

2. Enter "Aaron Judge" into the search box and click 🔍.

3. Select your book cover to see a list of related websites.

Glossary

adopted: To be adopted is to be officially taken in as part of a new family. Judge and his brother were adopted at a young age.

debut: A debut is when someone makes their first appearance. Judge made his MLB debut against the Tampa Bay Rays.

draft: Sports leagues use a draft to divide up the players who are new to the league. The Yankees selected Judge in the first round of the draft.

dugout: The dugout is where baseball players sit when they're not playing. Judge greeted his teammates by the dugout.

recruiting: Colleges use a recruiting process to persuade athletes to come play sports for them. Notre Dame was recruiting Judge to play college football.

repetition: Repetition is doing the same thing over and over. Repetition during batting practice helps Judge stay sharp.

rookie: A pro baseball player in his first full year is called a rookie. Judge was named the best rookie in the American League in 2017.

spring training: Spring training is when MLB teams hold practice sessions and games before the season starts. Judge had his first spring training with the Yankees in 2016.

Index

PHOTO CREDITS

The images in this book are reproduced through the courtesy of: Mark LoMoglio/Icon Sportswire/ AP Images, front cover (center); Lynne Sladky/AP Images, front cover (right), p.3; EFKS/ Shutterstock Images, front cover (stadium); Marcio Jose Bastos Silva/Shutterstock Images, front cover (field); Kathy Willens/AP Images, pp. 4–5; Bill Kostroun/AP Images, pp. 6, 8–9; eddtoro/ Shutterstock Images, p. 8; Joseph Sohm/Shutterstock Images, pp. 10–11; wavebreakmedia/ Shutterstock Images, p. 12; Frank Franklin II/AP Images, p. 13; Red Line Editorial, pp. 14, 27; Brian Westerholt/Four Seam Images/AP Images, p. 15; lev radin/Shutterstock Images, p. 16; John Froschauer/AP Images, pp. 16–17; Ron Schwane/AP Images, p. 18; Bekshon/Shutterstock Images, p. 20; Peter Joneleit/Cal Sport Media/AP Images, pp. 20–21; stockelements/ Shutterstock Images, p. 22 (left); RG-vc/Shutterstock Images, pp. 22 (right), 27 (right); Charles Krupa/AP Images, p. 23; Kyodo/AP Images, pp. 24–25; Elise Amendola/AP Images, p. 26; Africa Studios/Shutterstock Images, pp. 27 (left), 30.

ABOUT THE AUTHOR

Anthony K. Hewson is a freelance writer originally from San Diego, now living in the Bay Area with his wife and their two dogs.